I0880611

NORTHERN LIGHTS CROCHET

10 PROJECTS
INSPIRED BY
ICELAND'S BEAUTY

LEISURE ARTS, INC. • Maumelle, Arkansas

CONTENTS

ALIDA COWL

BASIC

SIZE

Finished Circumference:
About 26" (66 cm)

Finished Height:
About $8^1/_2$" (21.5 cm)

GAUGE

$6^1/_2$ single crochet = about 4" (10 cm) over pattern.

BE SURE TO CHECK YOUR GAUGE.

SHOPPING LIST

SUPER BULKY 6

Yarn (Super Bulky Weight)
LION BRAND® GO FOR FAUX™
(Art. #322)
☐ #098 Baked Alaska - 1 ball

Crochet Hook
LION BRAND® crochet hook
☐ Size N (10 mm)
or size needed for gauge

Additional Supply
☐ LION BRAND® large-eyed blunt needle

NOTES

1. The Cowl is crocheted in one piece in the round.
2. Due to the lush fur texture of this yarn, you may not be able to see your stitches. We found it easiest to feel for the next stitch.
3. If you'd like to keep the yarn contained as you work, slip the ball into a zippered plastic bag. Zip the bag closed, leaving an opening for the strand of yarn.

COWL

Chain 43.

Set-Up Row: Single crochet in the 2nd chain from the hook and in each chain across – you will have 42 single crochet in this row. Join with a slip stitch in top of the beginning chain to begin working in the round.

Round 1: Chain 1, single crochet in each stitch around; join with a slip stitch in top of the beginning chain.

Repeat Round 1 until almost all yarn has been used.

You don't need to end exactly at the end of a round – this yarn is very stretchy and it won't show if you stop crocheting at any point in a round.

Fasten off.

FINISHING

Thread ending yarn tail into the blunt needle, then weave through stitches on the inside of the Cowl to secure the yarn end. Thread beginning yarn tail into the blunt needle and sew the beginning and the end of the Set-Up Row together, then finish weaving in the tail.

TIP

On each round, count your stitches as you work around. This way, if you miss working into a stitch, you can simply make an extra stitch into the edge of the Cowl to keep your total number of stitches consistent.

VIVECA TOP

INTERMEDIATE

SIZES

S-L{1X-2X}

Finished Bust:
About 52{63}"/132{160} cm

Finished Front Length:
About 22{23}"/56{58.5} cm

Finished Back Length:
About 28{29}"/71{73.5} cm

Note: Pattern is written for smaller size with changes for larger size in braces. When only one number is given, it applies to both sizes. To follow pattern more easily, circle all numbers pertaining to your size before beginning.

GAUGE

14 sts and 7 rows = about 4" (10 cm) in Mesh and Cluster pattern.

BE SURE TO CHECK YOUR GAUGE.

SHOPPING LIST

MEDIUM 4

Yarn (Medium Weight)
LION BRAND® POUND OF LOVE® (Art. #550)
☐ #150 Oxford Grey - 1{2} ball(s)

Crochet Hook
LION BRAND® crochet hook
☐ Size J-10 (6 mm)
or size needed for gauge

Additional Supplies
☐ LION BRAND® stitch markers
☐ LION BRAND® large-eyed blunt needle

NOTES

1. Top is worked in 2 pieces: Back and Front.
2. Each piece is worked back and forth in rows, beg at lower edge. The Back is worked in Mesh and Cluster pattern. Front is worked same as Back, with Cable pattern worked in the center of the Mesh and Cluster pattern.
3. The Back is designed to be longer than the Front.
4. When you see 'work in pattern as established' in the instructions, this means to work the next row of the pattern sts, lining up sts as in previous rows.
5. For those who find visuals helpful, we've included stitch diagrams on page 15.

STITCH GUIDE

FPDC (front post double crochet)
Yarn over, insert hook from front to back then to front, going around post of indicated st, draw up a loop, (yarn over and draw through 2 loops on hook) twice.

BPTR (back post treble crochet)
Yarn over twice, insert hook from back to front then to back, going around post of indicated st, draw up a loop, (yarn over and draw through 2 loops on hook) 3 times.

FPTR (front post treble crochet)
Yarn over twice, insert hook from front to back then to front, going around post of indicated st, draw up a loop, (yarn over and draw through 2 loops on hook) 3 times.

3/3 FPTR-LC (3 over 3 front post treble crochet left cross)
Sk next 3 sts, FPTR around each of next 3 sts; working in front of the 3 sts just made, FPTR around each of the 3 skipped sts.

3/3 FPTR-RC (3 over 3 front post treble crochet right cross)
Sk next 3 sts, FPTR around each of next 3 sts; working behind the 3 sts just made, FPTR around each of the 3 skipped sts.

Cl (3 double crochet cluster)
Yarn over, insert hook in indicated st or sp, yarn over and draw up a loop, yarn over and draw through 2 loops on hook (2 loops rem on hook), (yarn over, insert hook in same st, yarn over and draw up a loop, yarn over and draw through 2 loops on hook) twice; yarn over and draw through all 4 loops on hook.

dc2tog-over-3 (dc 2 together worked over 3 sts)
Yarn over, insert hook in next st and draw up a loop, yarn over and draw through 2 loops, sk next st (the skipped st could be a ch-1 sp or Cl), yarn over, insert hook in next st and draw up a loop, yarn over and draw through 2 loops, yarn over and draw through all 3 loops on hook – 2 sts decreased.

PATTERN STITCHES

Cable Pattern (worked over 9 sts)
Row 1 (WS): BPTR around each of next 9 sts.
Row 2: FPTR-RC, FPDC around each of next 3 sts.
Row 3: BPTR around each of next 9 sts.
Row 4: FPDC around each of next 3 sts, FPTR-LC.
Row 5: BPTR around each of next 9 sts.
Rep Rows 2-5 for Cable pattern.

Mesh and Cluster Pattern
Row 1 (WS): Ch 4 (counts as dc, ch 1), turn, sk first ch-1 sp, dc in next dc, *(ch 1, sk next ch-1 sp, dc in next dc) to 1 ch-1 sp before next Cl, Cl in next ch-1 sp, dc in next dc, ch 1, sk next Cl, dc in next dc, Cl in next ch-1 sp, dc in next dc; rep from * until all Cl have been worked over, (ch 1, sk next ch-1 sp, dc in next dc) to beg ch-sp, ch 1, sk first ch of beg ch-sp, dc in next ch.
Row 2: Ch 4 (counts as dc, ch 1), turn, sk first ch-1 sp, dc in next dc, *(ch 1, sk next ch-1 sp, dc in next dc) to next Cl, ch 1, sk next Cl, dc in next dc, Cl in next ch-1 sp, dc in next dc, ch 1, sk next Cl, dc in next dc; rep from * until all Cl have been worked over, (ch 1, sk next ch-1 sp, dc in next dc) to beg ch-sp, ch 1, dc in 3rd ch of beg ch-4.
Rep Rows 1 and 2 for Mesh and Cluster pattern.

BACK

Ch 94{114}.
Set Up Row (RS): Dc in 6th ch from hook (5 skipped chains count as 1 base ch, dc, ch 1), (ch 1, sk next ch, dc in next ch) 3{2} times, *Cl in next ch, dc in next ch, (ch 1, sk next ch, dc in next ch) 8{7} times; rep from * 3{5} more times, Cl in next ch, dc in next ch, (ch 1, sk next ch, dc in next ch) 4{3} times – you will have 46{56} dc, 40{48} ch-1 sps, and 5{7} Cl in this row.

Beg with Row 1 of pattern, work in Mesh and Cluster pattern until piece measures about 16" (40.5 cm) from beg, end with a WS row as the last row you work.

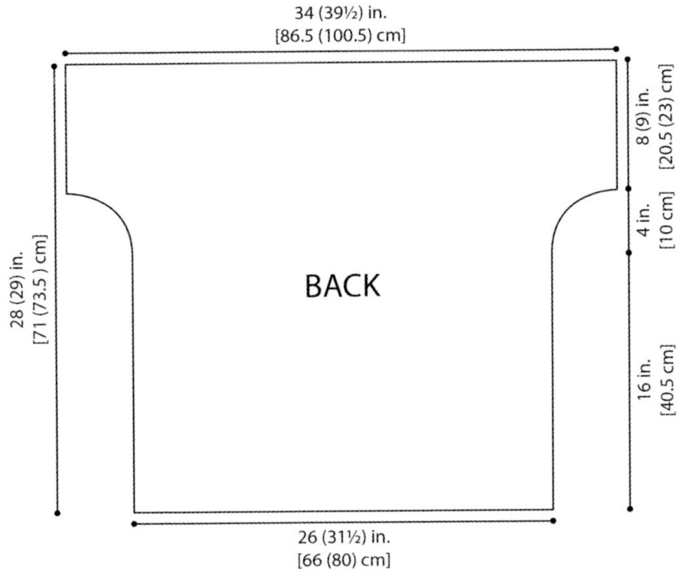
34 (39½) in.
[86.5 (100.5) cm]
BACK
28 (29) in.
[71 (73.5) cm]
8 (9) in.
[20.5 (23) cm]
4 in.
[10 cm]
16 in.
[40.5 cm]
26 (31½) in.
[66 (80) cm]

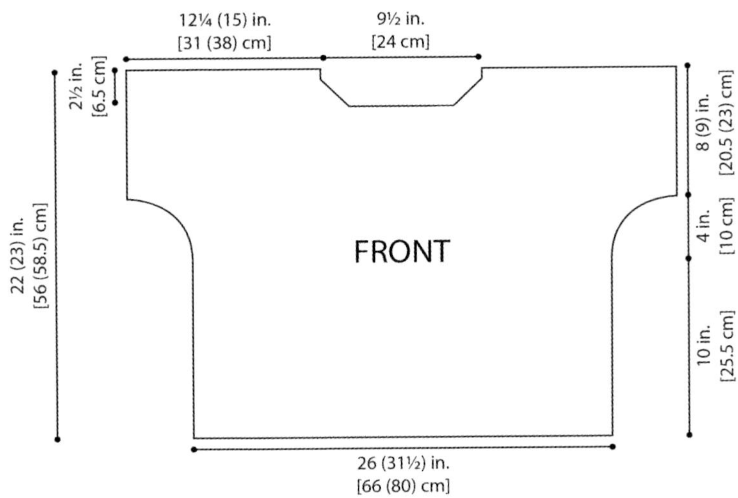
12¼ (15) in.
[31 (38) cm]
9½ in.
[24 cm]
2½ in.
[6.5 cm]
FRONT
22 (23) in.
[56 (58.5) cm]
8 (9) in.
[20.5 (23) cm]
4 in.
[10 cm]
10 in.
[25.5 cm]
26 (31½) in.
[66 (80) cm]

Shape Armholes

Row 1 (Increase Row – RS): Ch 4 (counts as dc, ch 1), turn, dc in first dc (increase made), work in Mesh and Cluster pattern as established to beg ch-sp, ch 1, (dc, ch 1, dc) in 3rd ch of beg ch-4 (increase made) – 48{58} dc, 42{50} ch-1 sps, and 5{7} Cl.

Rows 2-6: Rep Row 1 for 5 more times – 58{68} dc, 47{53} ch-1 sps, and 10{14} Cl in Row 6.

Row 7: Ch 4 (counts as dc, ch 1), turn, dc in first dc, ch 1, sk first ch-1 sp, dc in next dc, Cl in next ch-1 sp, dc in next dc, ch 1, sk next ch-1 sp, dc in next dc, continue in Mesh and Cluster pattern as established to last 2 ch-sps, Cl in next ch-1 sp, dc in next dc, ch 1, (dc, ch 1, dc) in 3rd ch of beg ch-4 – 60{70} dc, 52{60} ch-1 sps, and 7{9} Cl.

Place a marker at beg and end of last row worked.

Work in Mesh and Cluster pattern as established until armholes measure about 8{9}"/20.5{23} cm from markers. Remove markers. Fasten off.

FRONT

Ch 94{114}.

Set-Up Row (RS): Dc in 6th ch from hook (5 skipped chains count as 1 base ch, dc, ch 1), (ch 1, sk next ch, dc in next ch) 3{2} times, *Cl in next ch, dc in next ch, (ch 1, sk next ch, dc in next ch) 8{7} times; rep from * 0{1} more time(s), Cl in next ch, dc in next ch, (ch 1, sk next ch, dc in next ch) 6{5} times, ch 1, sk next ch; dc in next 2 ch and place a marker in the first of the 2 dc just made, 2 dc in next ch, dc in next ch, 2 dc in next ch, dc in next 2 ch and place a marker in the last dc just made; (ch 1, sk next ch, dc in next ch) 7{6} times, **Cl in next ch, dc in next ch, (ch 1, sk next ch, dc in next ch) 8{7} times; rep from ** 0{1} more time(s), Cl in next ch, dc in next ch, (ch 1, sk next ch, dc in next ch) 4{3} times – you will have 9 sts between markers for Cable pattern (including marked sts), with 21{26} dc, 19{23} ch-1 sps, and 2{3} Cl on each side of Cable pattern.

Move markers up as each row is worked.

Row 1: Work Row 1 of Mesh and Cluster pattern as follows: Ch 4 (counts as dc, ch 1), turn, sk first ch-1 sp, dc in next dc, (ch 1, sk next ch-1 sp, dc in next dc) to ch-1 sp before next Cl, *Cl in next ch-1 sp, dc in next dc, ch 1, sk next Cl, dc in next dc, Cl in next ch-1 sp, dc in next dc, (ch 1, sk next ch-1 sp, dc in next dc) to ch-1 sp before next Cl; rep from * to ch-1 sp before first marker; beg in first marked st, work Row 1 of Cable pattern over next 9 sts working last Cable pattern st in 2nd marked st; continue Row 1 of Mesh and Cluster pattern as follows: **(Ch 1, sk next ch-1 sp, dc in next dc) to ch-1 sp before next Cl, Cl in next ch-1 sp, dc in next dc, ch 1, sk next Cl, dc in next dc, Cl in next ch-1 sp, dc in next dc; rep from ** until all Cl have been worked over, (ch 1, sk next ch-1 sp, dc in next dc) to beg ch-sp, ch 1, sk first ch of beg ch-sp, dc in next ch – 21{26} dc, 17{20} ch-1 sps, and 4{6} Cl on each side of Cable pattern.

Row 2: Work in Mesh and Cluster pattern as established to first marker; beg in first marked st, work next row of Cable pattern over next 9 sts working last Cable pattern st in 2nd marked st; work in Mesh and Cluster pattern as established to end of row.

Rep Row 2 until piece measures about 10" (25.5 cm) from beg, end with a WS row as the last row you work.

Shape Armholes

Row 1 (Increase Row – RS): Ch 4 (counts as dc, ch 1), turn, dc in first dc (increase made), work in Mesh and Cluster pattern as established to first marker; beg in first marked st, work next row of Cable pattern over next 9 sts working last Cable pattern st in 2nd marked st; work in Mesh and Cluster pattern as established to beg ch-sp, ch 1, (dc, ch 1, dc) in 3rd ch of beg ch-4 (increase made) – 22{27} dc, 20{24} ch-1 sps, and 2{3} Cl on each side of Cable pattern.

Note: When you see '0' repeats in an instruction, this means that for that size, you should not work any sts, just skip to the next part of the instruction.

Rows 2-6: Rep Row 1 for 5 more times – 27{32} dc, 23{26} ch-1 sps, and 4{6} Cl on each side of Cable pattern in Row 6.
Row 7: Ch 4 (counts as dc, ch 1), turn, dc in first dc, ch 1, sk first ch-1 sp, dc in next dc, Cl in next ch-1 sp, dc in next dc, ch 1, sk next ch-1 sp, dc in next dc, continue in Mesh and Cluster pattern as established to first marker; beg in first marked st, work next row of Cable pattern over next 9 sts working last Cable pattern st in 2nd marked st; work in Mesh and Cluster pattern as established to last 2 ch-sps, Cl in next ch-1 sp, dc in next dc, ch 1, (dc, ch 1, dc) in 3rd ch of beg ch-4 – 28{33} dc, 25{29} ch-1 sps, and 3{4} Cl on each side of Cable pattern.

Place a marker at beg and end of last row worked.

Row 8 (WS): Work in Mesh and Cluster pattern as established to first marker; beg in first marked st, work next row of Cable pattern over next 9 sts working last Cable pattern st in 2nd marked st; work in Mesh and Cluster pattern as established to end of row – 28{33} dc, 22{25} ch-1 sps, and 6{8} Cl on each side of Cable pattern.

Rep Row 8, working in Mesh and Cluster pattern as established and keeping sts between markers in Cable pattern as established, until piece measures about 5½{6½}"/14{16.5} cm from armhole markers, end with a WS row as the last row you work.

Shape Neck

From RS, place a marker in the 5th dc before first Cable pattern marker and place another marker in the 4th dc following last Cable pattern marker.
Remove Cable pattern markers.

Left Shoulder

Row 1 (RS): Work in Mesh and Cluster pattern as established to first marker, beg in marked st, dc2tog-over-3, remove marker; leave rem sts unworked for right shoulder – 24{29} dc, 20{24} ch-1 sps, and 3{4}Cl.
Row 2: Ch 3 (does not count as a st), turn, sk first ch-1 sp, dc in next dc, work in Mesh and Cluster pattern as established to end of row – 23{28} dc, 16{20} ch-1 sps, and 6{7} Cl.
Row 3: Work in Mesh and Cluster pattern as established to last 3 sts, dc2tog-over-3 – 22{27} dc, 18{23} ch-1 sps, and 3{3} Cl.
Row 4: Ch 3 (counts as dc), turn, work in Mesh and Cluster pattern as established to end of row – 22{27} dc, 16{19} ch-1 sps, and 5{7} Cl.
Fasten off.

Right Shoulder

Row 1 (RS): From RS, draw up a loop in rem marked dc, ch 3 (does not count as a st), sk next ch-1 sp, dc in next dc, work in Mesh and Cluster pattern as established to end of row – 24{29} dc, 20{24} ch-1 sps, and 3{4} Cl.
Row 2: Work in Mesh and Cluster pattern as established to last 3 sts, dc2tog-over-3 – 23{28} dc, 16{20} ch-1 sps, and 6{7} Cl.

Row 3: Ch 3 (does not count as a st), turn, sk next ch-1 sp, dc in next dc, work in Mesh and Cluster pattern as established to end of row – 22{27} dc, 18{23} ch-1 sps, and 3{3} Cl.

Row 4: Work in Mesh and Cluster pattern as established to last 3 sts, dc2tog-over-3 – 22{27} dc, 16{19} ch-1 sps, and 5{7} Cl.
Fasten off.

FINISHING

Sew shoulder seams.
Sew side seams.

Neck Edging

From RS, join yarn with a sl st in either shoulder seam, sc evenly spaced around neck edge; join with sl st in first sc.
Fasten off.

Weave in ends.

Cable Pattern

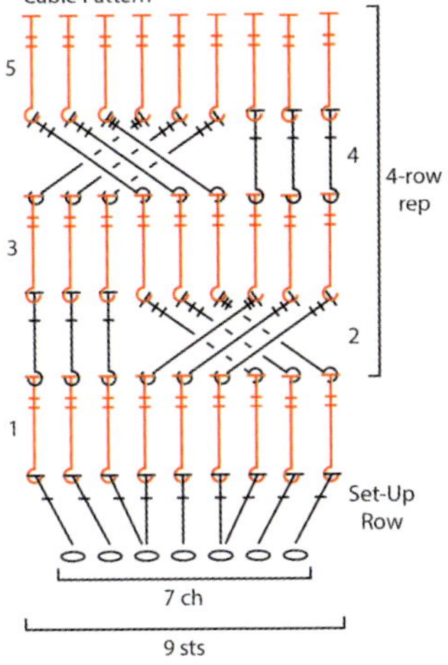

Mesh and Cluster Pattern

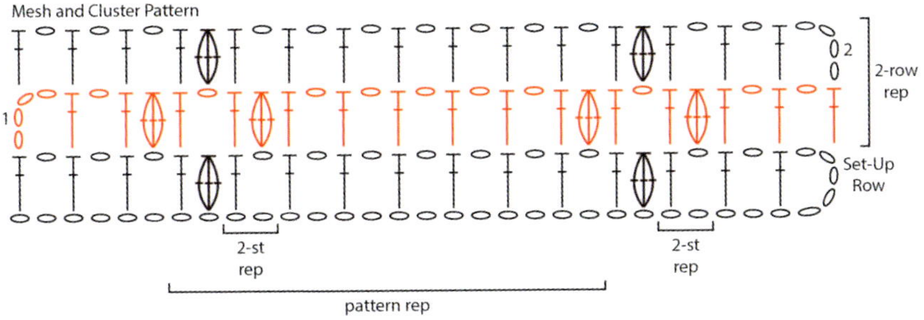

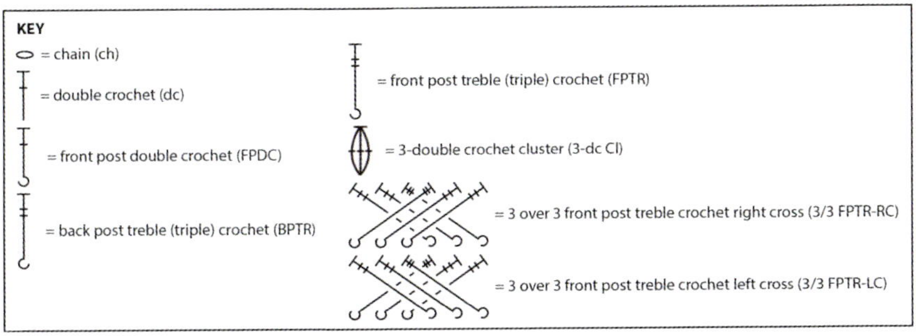

ULLA TOP

EASY

SIZES

S-L{1X-3X}

Finished Width:
About 66{76}"/157.5{193} cm

Finished Length:
About 26{27}"/66{68.5} cm, not including cowl neck.

Note: Pattern is written for smallest size with changes for larger size in braces. When only one number is given, it applies to both sizes. To follow pattern more easily, circle all numbers pertaining to your size before beginning.

GAUGE

12 hdc = about 4¾" (12 cm) with smaller hook and A.
12 hdc = about 4½" (11.5 cm); 10 rows = about 4" (10 cm) with smaller hook and B.

BE SURE TO CHECK YOUR GAUGE.

SHOPPING LIST

Yarn (Bulky Weight) BULKY 5
LION BRAND® HOMESPUN® (Art. #790)
☐ #600 Clouds - 3{4} skeins (A)

(Medium Weight) MEDIUM 4
LION BRAND® HEARTLAND®
☐ #149 Great Smoky Mountains - 3{4} balls (B)

Crochet Hook
LION BRAND® crochet hook
☐ Size K-10.5 (6.5 mm) **or** size needed for gauge

Additional Supplies
☐ LION BRAND® large-eyed blunt needle
☐ Crochet hook size L-11 (8 mm)

NOTES

1. Top is made from 2 identical pieces: Back and Front.
2. Front and Back each begin with a center panel worked from lower edge. Side panels are worked along side edges of center panel.
3. Stitches are picked up around the neck edge to work cowl neck in the round.

STITCH GUIDE

hdc2tog (hdc 2 sts together)
(Yarn over, insert hook in next st and draw up a loop) twice, yarn over and draw through all 5 loops on hook – 1 st decreased.

BACK

Center Panel
With smaller hook and A, ch 34{47}.
Row 1 (RS): Sc in 2nd ch from hook and in each ch across – you will have 33{46} sc.
Row 2: Ch 2 (counts as hdc), turn, sk first st, hdc in each st across.
Row 3: Ch 2 (counts as hdc), turn, sk first st, hdc in each st across working last hdc in top of beg ch-2.
Rep Row 3 until piece measures about 26{27}"/66{68.5} cm from beg.
Fasten off.

First Side Panel
Note: If you are right-handed this panel is worked along the right side edge of the center panel. If you are left-handed this panel is worked along the left side edge of the center panel.

From RS with smaller hook, join B with a sl st in lower corner of center panel so that you are ready to work along one long side edge.

Row 1 (RS): Ch 1, work 70{73} sc evenly spaced along side edge.
Row 2: Ch 2 (counts as hdc), turn, sk first st, hdc in each st across.
Row 3: Ch 2 (counts as hdc), turn, sk first st, hdc in each st across, working last hdc in top of beg ch-2.
Row 4 (Decrease Row – WS): Ch 2 (counts as hdc), turn, sk first st, hdc2tog, hdc in each st across, working last hdc in top of beg ch-2 – 69{72} hdc.
Row 5 (Decrease Row – RS): Ch 2 (counts as hdc), turn, sk first st, hdc in each st to last 3 sts, hdc2tog, hdc in top of beg ch-2 – 68{71} sts.
Rows 6-25: Rep Rows 4 and 5 for 10 more times – 48{51} sts in Row 25.
Fasten off.

Second Side Panel
Note: If you are right-handed this panel is worked along the left side edge of the center panel. If you are left-handed this panel is worked along the right side edge of the center panel.

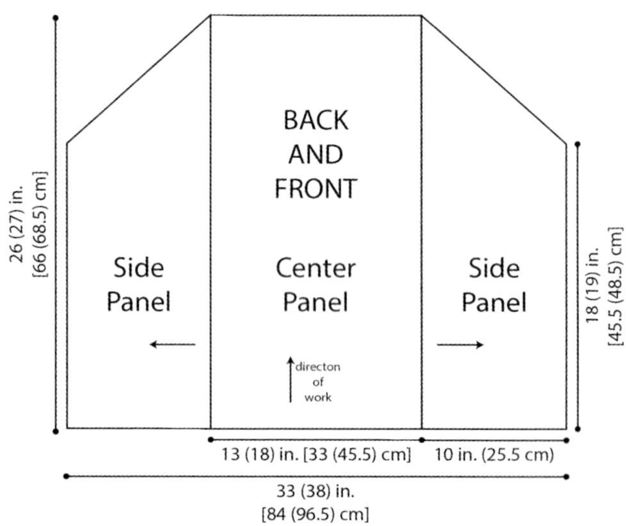

From RS with smaller hook, join B with a sl st in upper corner of center panel so that you are ready to work along the remaining long side edge.

Row 1 (RS): Ch 1, work 70{73} sc evenly spaced along side edge.
Row 2: Ch 2 (counts as hdc), turn, sk first st, hdc in each st across.
Row 3: Ch 2 (counts as hdc), turn, sk first st, hdc in each st across working last hdc in top of beg ch-2.
Row 4 (Decrease Row – WS): Ch 2 (counts as hdc), turn, sk first st, hdc in each st to last 3 sts, hdc2tog, hdc in top of beg ch-2 – 69{72} sts.
Row 5 (Decrease Row – RS): Ch 2 (counts as hdc), turn, sk first st, hdc2tog, hdc in each st across, working last hdc in top of beg ch-2 – 68{71} hdc.
Rows 6-25: Rep Rows 4 and 5 for 10 more times – 48{51} sts in Row 25.
Fasten off.

FRONT

Make same as Back.

FINISHING

Sew shoulder seams, leaving center 10{11}"/25.5{28} cm open for neck.

Cowl Neck

From RS with smaller hook, join A with a sl st in either shoulder seam.

Rnd 1: Ch 2 (counts as hdc), work 26{28} hdc evenly spaced along neck edge to next shoulder seam, work 26{28} hdc evenly spaced along neck edge to beg of rnd; join with sl st in top of beg ch-2 – 52{56} hdc.
Rnds 2-6: Ch 2 (counts as hdc), hdc in next st and each st around; join with sl st in top of beg ch-2.

Change to larger hook.

Rnds 7-13: Ch 2 (counts as hdc), hdc in next st and each st around; join with sl st in top of beg ch-2.
Fasten off.

Sew side edges of Front and Back together beg at lower corners and leaving about 9{10}"/23{25.5} cm unsewn for armholes.

Weave in ends.

DALLA AFGHAN

EASY

SIZE

About 48" x 60" (122 cm x 152.5 cm)

GAUGE

1 Square = about 12" x 12"
(30.5 cm x 30.5 cm).

BE SURE TO CHECK YOUR GAUGE.

SHOPPING LIST

LIGHT 3

Yarn (Light Weight)
LION BRAND® MANDALA® BABY
(Art. #526)

- ☐ #204 Wishing Well - 1 cake (A)
- ☐ #205 Echo Caves - 1 cake (B)

LION BRAND® MANDALA®
(Art. #525)

- ☐ #219 Brownie - 1 cake (C)
- ☐ #221 Harpy - 1 cake (D)
- ☐ #223 Mermaid - 1 cake (E)

Crochet Hook
LION BRAND® crochet hook

- ☐ Size H-8 (5 mm)
  or size needed for gauge

Additional Supply

- ☐ LION BRAND® large-eyed blunt needle

NOTES

1. 20 Squares are worked separately, then sewn together to make the Afghan.

2. Each Square is worked in joined rnds with RS always facing.

3. Each Square begins as a circle, then the following rnds shape the circle into a square.

4. For those who find a visual helpful, we've included a stitch diagram of the more complicated last 5 rnds on page 25.

SQUARES

(make 20 – 4 each with A, B, C, D, and E)
Wrap yarn around index finger. Insert hook into ring on finger, yarn over and draw up a loop. Carefully slip ring from finger and work the stitches of Rnd 1 into the ring.

Rnd 1: Ch 3 (counts as dc), work 11 dc in ring; join with sl st in top of beg ch – you will have 12 dc in this rnd. Gently but firmly, pull tail to tighten center of ring.

Rnd 2: Ch 3 (counts as dc), dc in same st as joining sl st, work 2 dc in each st around; join with sl st in top of beg ch – 24 dc.

Rnd 3: Ch 3 (counts as dc), 2 dc in next st, *dc in next st, 2 dc in next st; rep from * around; join with sl st in top of beg ch – 36 dc.

Rnd 4: Ch 3 (counts as dc), dc in next st, 2 dc in next st, *dc in next 2 sts, 2 dc in next st; rep from * around; join with sl st in top of beg ch – 48 dc.

Rnd 5: Ch 3 (counts as dc), dc in next 2 sts, 2 dc in next st, *dc in next 3 sts, 2 dc in next st; rep from * around; join with sl st in top of beg ch – 60 dc.

Rnd 6: Ch 3 (counts as dc), dc in next 3 sts, 2 dc in next st, *dc in next 4 sts, 2 dc in next st; rep from * around; join with sl st in top of beg ch – 72 dc.

Rnd 7: Ch 3 (counts as dc), dc in next 4 sts, 2 dc in next st, *dc in next 5 sts, 2 dc in next st; rep from * around; join with sl st in top of beg ch – 84 dc.

Rnd 8: Ch 3 (counts as dc), dc in next 5 sts, 2 dc in next st, *dc in next 6 sts, 2 dc in next st; rep from * around; join with sl st in top of beg ch – 96 dc.

Rnd 9: Ch 3 (counts as dc), dc in next 6 sts, 2 dc in next st, *dc in next 7 sts, 2 dc in next st; rep from * around; join with sl st in top of beg ch – 108 dc.

Rnd 10: Ch 5 (counts as tr, ch 1), 2 tr in same st as joining sl st, *tr in next 3 sts, dc in next 3 sts, hdc in next 3 sts, sc in next 8 sts, hdc in next 3 sts, dc in next 3 sts, tr in next 3 sts, (2 tr, ch 1, 2 tr) in next st for corner; rep from * 2 more times, tr in next 3 sts, dc in next 3 sts, hdc in next 3 sts, sc in next 8 sts, hdc in next 3 sts, dc in next 3 sts, tr in next 3 sts, tr in base of beg ch-5; join with sl st in 4th ch of beg ch-5 (first corner complete) – 120 sts and 4 corner ch-1 sps.

Rnd 11: Sl st in first corner ch-sp, ch 5 (counts as tr, ch 1), 2 tr in same ch-sp, *tr in next 2 sts, dc in next 3 sts, hdc in next 3 sts, sc in next 14 sts, hdc in next 3 sts, dc in next 3 sts, tr in next 2 sts, (2 tr, ch 1, 2 tr) in next corner ch-1 sp; rep from * 2 more times, tr in next 2 sts, dc in next 3 sts, hdc in next 3 sts, sc in next 14 sts, hdc in next 3 sts, dc in next 3 sts, tr in next 2 sts, tr again in first corner ch-sp; join with sl st in 4th ch of beg ch-5 – 136 sts and 4 corner ch-1 sps.

Rnd 12: Sl st in first corner ch-sp, ch 5 (counts as tr, ch 1), 2 tr in same ch-sp, *dc in next 8 sts, hdc in next 18 sts, dc in next 8 sts, (2 tr, ch 1, 2 tr) in next corner ch-1 sp; rep from * 2 more times, dc in next 8 sts, hdc in next 18 sts, dc in next 8 sts, tr again in first corner ch-sp; join with sl st in 4th ch of beg ch-5 – 152 sts and 4 corner ch-1 sps.

Rnd 13: Ch 1, *3 sc in next corner ch-1 sp, sc in each st to next corner ch-1 sp; rep from * 3 more times; join with sl st in first sc – 164 sc.

Fasten off.

FINISHING

Arrange Squares into 4 strips of 5 Squares each. Place the colors however you fancy! Sew Squares into strips, then sew strips together to make the Afghan.

Weave in ends.

KEY

- ● = slip stitch (sl st)
- ⬭ = chain (ch)
- × = single crochet (sc)
- T = half double crochet (hdc)
- = double crochet (dc)
- = treble crochet (tr)

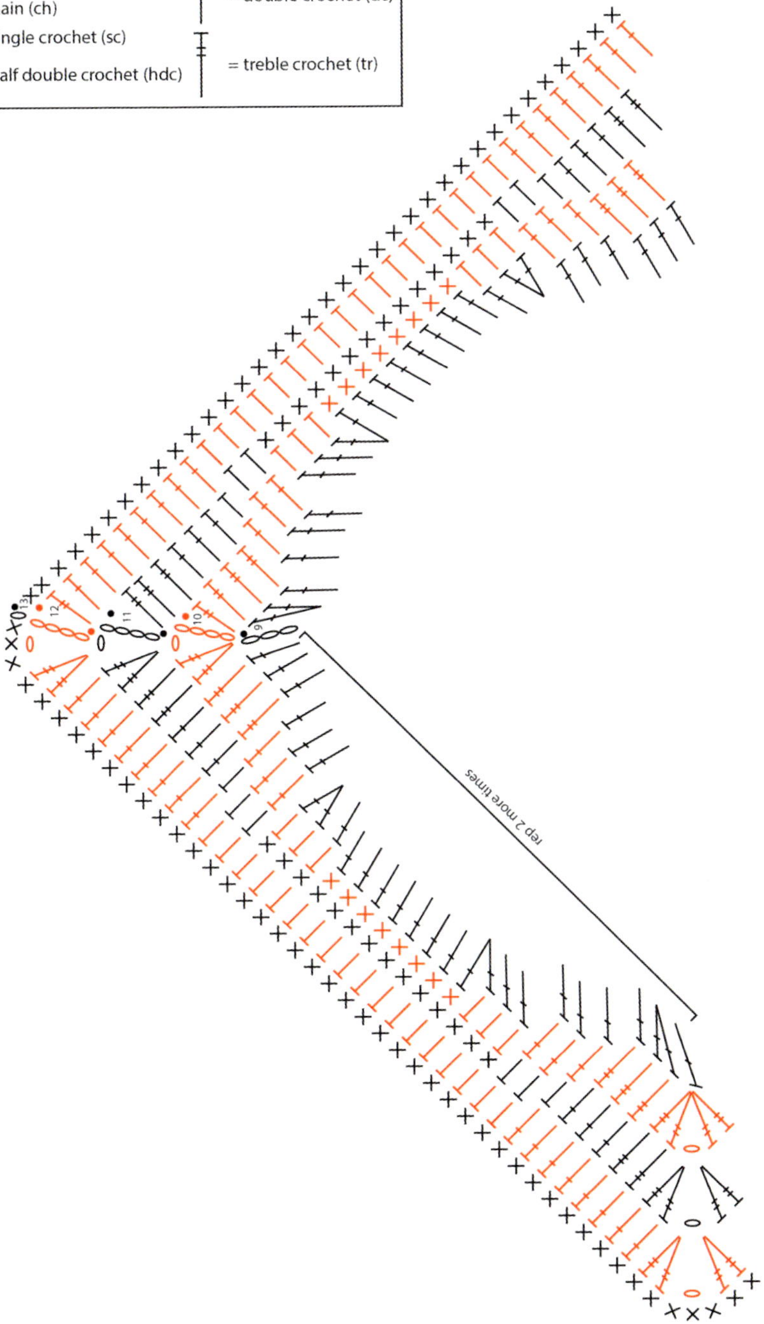

CARINA CARDIGAN

EASY

SIZES

S{M/L, 1X, 2X}

Finished Chest:
38{43, 48, 53}"/
96.5{109, 122, 134.5} cm

Finished Length:
26½{27½, 28½, 29½}"/
67.5{70, 72.5, 75} cm

Note Pattern is written for smallest size with changes for larger sizes in braces. When only one number is given, it applies to all sizes. To follow pattern more easily, circle all numbers pertaining to your size before beginning.

GAUGE

7 sts (2⅓ V-sts) = about 3"(7.5 cm);
4 rows = about 4¼" (11 cm)
in V-st pattern.

BE SURE TO CHECK YOUR GAUGE.

SHOPPING LIST

Yarn (Super Bulky Weight) SUPER BULKY 6
LION BRAND® HOMETOWN USA® (Art. #135)

☐ #302 Aspen Tweed - 13{15, 17, 19} balls

Crochet Hook
LION BRAND® crochet hook

☐ Size N (10 mm) **or** size needed for gauge

Additional Supply

☐ LION BRAND® large-eyed blunt needle

STITCH GUIDE

V-st (Dc, ch 1, dc) in indicated st or sp.

NOTES

1. Cardigan is worked in 6 pieces: Back, 2 Fronts, 2 Sleeves and Front Bands/Collar.
2. Back, Fronts and Sleeves are worked in an easy V-st pattern. The 2 Fronts are worked the same, the pattern stitch is reversible so simply flip one Front over so that it is the mirror image of the other Front.
3. Front Bands/Collar and optional Belt are worked in sc.
4. For those who find visuals helpful, we've included stitch diagrams on page 27.

PATTERN STITCH

V-st Pattern (multiple of 3 sts)

Row 1: V-st in 6th ch from hook (5 skipped ch count as 2 base ch and dc), sk next 2 ch, *V-st in next ch, sk next 2 ch; rep from * to last ch, dc in last ch.

Row 2: Ch 3 (counts as first dc), turn, V-st in ch-1 sp of each V-st across, dc in top of beg-ch.

Rep Row 2 for V-st pattern.

BACK

Ch 48{54, 60, 66}.

Row 1: Work Row 1 of V-st pattern – 14{16, 18, 20} V-sts and 1 dc at each end of row.

Continue in V-st pattern for 16 {16, 17, 17} more rows.

Fasten off.

Shape Armholes

Row 1: Turn, join yarn with a sl st in 2nd dc of first V-st, ch 3 (counts as first dc), V-st in ch-1 sp of each V-st across to last V-st, dc in first dc of last V-st; leave rem sts unworked – 12{14, 16, 18} V-sts and 1 dc at each end of row.

Continue in V-st pattern for 7{8, 8, 9} more rows.

Fasten off.

FRONTS (MAKE 2)

Ch 21{24, 27, 30}.

Row 1: Work Row 1 of V-st pattern – 5{6, 7, 8} V-sts and 1 dc at each end of row.

Continue in V-st pattern for 16{16, 17, 17} more rows.

Do not fasten off.

Shape Armhole

Row 1: Ch 3, turn, V-st in ch-1 sp of each V-st across to last V-st, dc in first dc of last V-st; leave rem sts unworked – 4{5, 6, 7} V-sts and 1 dc at each end of row.

Continue in V-st pattern for 7{8, 8, 9} more rows.

Fasten off.

SLEEVES (MAKE 2)

Ch 24{24, 24, 27}.

Row 1: Work Row 1 of V-st pattern – 6{6, 6, 7} V-sts and 1 dc at each end of row.

Row 2 (Increase Row): Ch 3 (counts as first dc in this and all following rows), turn, dc in first dc, V-st in ch-1 sp of each V-st across, 2 dc in top of beg ch – 6{6, 6, 7} V-sts and 2 dc at each end of row.

Row 3 (Increase Row): Ch 3, turn, dc in first dc, dc in next dc, V-st in ch-1 sp of each V-st across, dc in next dc, 2 dc in top of beg ch – 6{6, 6, 7} V-sts and 3 dc at each end of row.

Row 4 (Increase Row): Ch 3, turn, V-st in next dc, V-st in ch-1 sp of each V-st across, sk 2nd dc of last V-st, sk next dc, V-st in next dc, dc in top of beg ch – 8{8, 8, 9} V-sts and 1 dc at each end of row.

Row 5: Ch 3, turn, V-st in ch-1 sp of each V-st across, dc in top of beg ch.

Rows 6 thru 13{17, 17, 17}: Rep Rows 2-5 for 2{3, 3, 3} more times – 12{14, 14, 15} V-sts and 1 dc at each end of row.

Continue in V-st pattern until piece measures about 18{19, 19, 20}"/45.5{48.5, 48.5, 51} cm from beg.

Fasten off.

FINISHING

Sew shoulder seams. Sew in Sleeves.
Sew side and Sleeve seams.

Sleeve Edging

From RS, join yarn with a sl st at wrist edge of one Sleeve.

Rnd 1: Ch 1, sc evenly spaced around edge; join with sl st in first sc.

Rnd 2: Ch 1, sc in each sc around; join with sl st in first sc.

Fasten off.

Rep edging on 2nd Sleeve.

Lower Edging

From RS, join yarn with a sl st in lower front corner so that you are ready to work across the lower edge of Cardigan.

Row 1: Ch 1, sc evenly spaced across lower edge of Cardigan.

Row 2: Ch 1, turn, sc in each sc across.

Fasten off.

Front Bands/Collar

Ch 11.

Row 1: Sc in 2nd ch from hook and in each ch across – 10 sc.

Row 2: Ch 1, turn, working in back loops only, sc in each sc across.

Rep Row 2 until piece measures about 57{59, 61, 63}"/145{150, 155, 160} cm and fits along Left Front edge, around Back neck, and along Right Front edge of Cardigan.

Fasten off. Sew in place.

Belt (optional)
Ch 4.
Row 1: Sc in 2nd ch from hook and in each ch across – 3 sc.
Row 2: Ch 1, turn, working in back loops only, sc in each sc across.
Rep Row 2 until piece measures about 60"{152.5 cm} from beg or desired length. Fasten off.

Weave in ends.

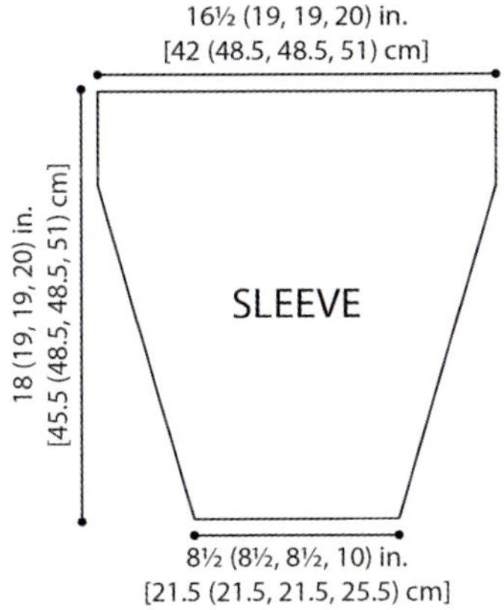

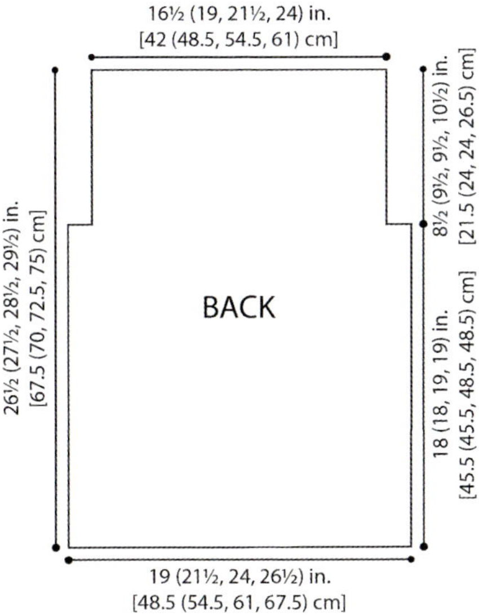

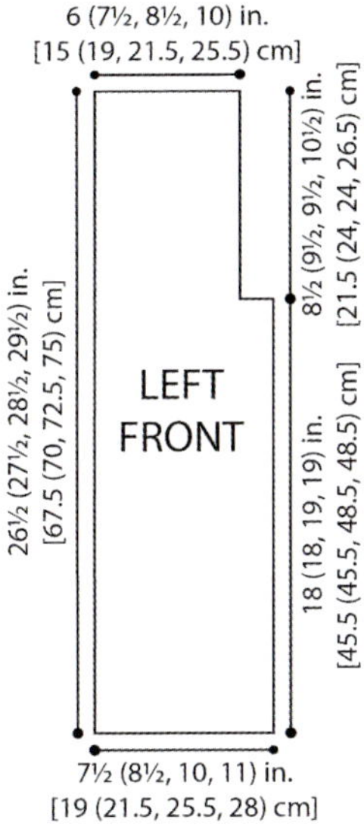

V-st Pattern

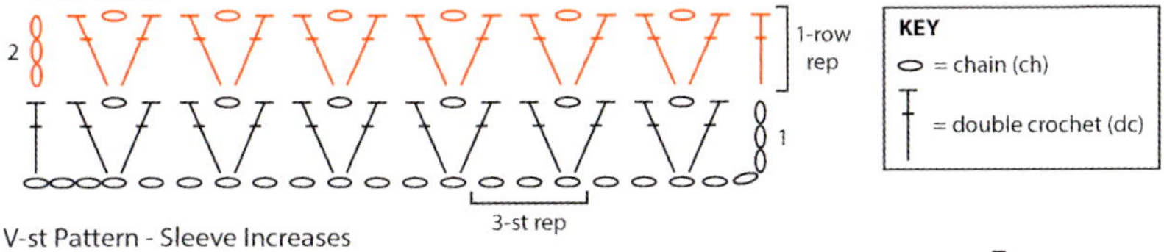

V-st Pattern - Sleeve Increases

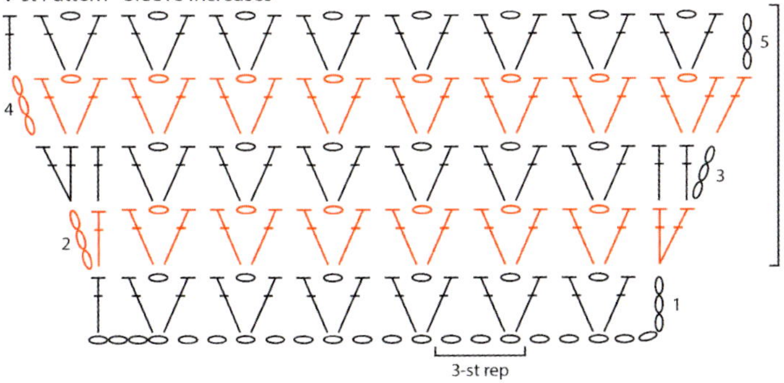

HEIGE HAT

EASY

SIZES

Finished Circumference:
About 20" (51 cm) will stretch to fit a range of sizes

Finished Height:
About 8" (20.5 cm)

GAUGE

11 hdc = about 4 " (10 cm).

BE SURE TO CHECK YOUR GAUGE.

SHOPPING LIST

Yarn (Bulky Weight) BULKY 5
LION BRAND®SCARFIE® (Art. #826)
☐ #206 Cream/Taupe - 1 ball

Crochet Hook
LION BRAND® crochet hook
☐ Size K-10.5 (6.5 mm)
or size needed for gauge

Additional Supply
☐ LION BRAND® large-eyed blunt needle

NOTES

1. Hat is worked in one piece in joined rnds, beginning at top of Hat.

2. All rnds in Bobble band are worked on WS. This becomes the RS when the band is folded up.

STITCH GUIDE

Bobble

Yarn over, insert hook in indicated st and draw up a loop, yarn over and draw through 2 loops on hook (2 loops rem on hook), (yarn over, insert hook in same st and draw up a loop, yarn over and draw through 2 loops on hook) 3 times (5 loops rem on hook), yarn over, draw through all loops on hook.

hdc2tog (hdc 2 sts together)

(Yarn over, insert hook in next st and draw up a loop) twice, yarn over and draw through all 5 loops on hook – 1 st decreased.

HAT

Ch 3.

Rnd 1 (RS): Work 8 hdc in 3rd ch from hook (2 skipped ch do not count as a st); join with sl st in first hdc – you will have 8 hdc.

Rnd 2: Ch 2 (does not count as a st), 2 hdc in each st around; join with sl st in first hdc – you will have 16 hdc at the end of this rnd.

Rnd 3: Ch 2 (does not count as a st), hdc in first st, 2 hdc in next st, *hdc in next st, 2 hdc in next st; rep from * around; join with sl st in first hdc – 24 hdc.

Rnd 4: Ch 2 (does not count as a st), hdc in first 2 sts, 2 hdc in next st, *hdc in next 2 sts, 2 hdc in next st; rep from * around; join with sl st in first hdc – 32 hdc.

Rnd 5: Ch 2 (does not count as a st), hdc in first 3 sts, 2 hdc in next st, *hdc in next 3 sts, 2 hdc in next st; rep from * around; join with sl st in first hdc – 40 hdc.

Rnd 6: Ch 2 (does not count as a st), hdc in first 4 sts, 2 hdc in next st, *hdc in next 4 sts, 2 hdc in next st; rep from * around; join with sl st in first hdc – 48 hdc.

Rnd 7: Ch 2 (does not count as a st), hdc in first 5 sts, 2 hdc in next st, *hdc in next 5 sts, 2 hdc in next st; rep from * around; join with sl st in first hdc – 56 hdc.

Rnds 8-19: Ch 2 (does not count as a st), hdc in each st around; join with sl st in first hdc.

Note: When you turn your work at the beginning of the Set-up Rnd, you will be working on the WS. You'll continue to work only on the WS (NOT turning) until all rnds of the Bobble Band are complete. This becomes the RS when the band is folded up.

Bobble Band

Set-Up Rnd (WS): Ch 1, TURN, working in back loops only, sc in each st around; join with sl st in beg ch-1 – 56 sc.

Rnd 1: Ch 3 (does not count as a st), do NOT turn, *Bobble in next st, dc in next st; rep from * around; join with sl st in top of beg ch-3 – 28 Bobbles and 28 dc.

Rnd 2: Ch 1, sc in each st around; join with sl st in beg ch-1 – 56 sc.

Rnd 3: Ch 3 (does not count as a st), *dc in next st, Bobble in next st; rep from * around; join with sl st in top of beg ch-3.

Rnd 4: Ch 1, sc in each st around; join with sl st in beg ch-1 – 56 sc.

Rnds 5 and 6: Rep Rnds 1 and 2.

Fasten off.

FINISHING

Weave in ends.

VASTI SHAWL

EASY

SIZE

About 32" x 68" (81.5 cm x 172.5 cm) at longest and widest points, not including fringe.

GAUGE

8 sts [two (3 dc, ch 1) groups] = about 3½" (9 cm);
7 rows = about 4½" (11.5 cm).

BE SURE TO CHECK YOUR GAUGE.

SHOPPING LIST

Yarn (Medium Weight) MEDIUM 4

LION BRAND® SHAWL IN A BALL® (Art. #828)

- ☐ #301 Moonstone - 1 ball (A)
- ☐ #300 Om Opal - 1 ball (B)

Crochet Hook

LION BRAND® crochet hook

- ☐ Size H-8 (5 mm) **or** size needed for gauge

Additional Supply

- ☐ LION BRAND® large-eyed blunt needle

NOTES

1. Shawl is worked in one piece, beginning at center of top edge, using two colors of yarn.

2. Increases are worked to shape the Shawl.

3. Fringe is added across the lower edge of the Shawl.

4. For those who find a visual helpful, we've included a stitch diagram on page 34.

SHAWL

With A, ch 5.

Row 1 (RS): (3 Dc, ch 2, 3 dc, ch 1, dc) in 5th ch from hook (4 skipped ch count as dc, ch 1) – you will have two 3-dc groups in this row.

Row 2: Ch 4 (counts as dc, ch 1), turn, 3 dc in first ch-1 sp, ch 1, (3 dc, ch 2, 3 dc) in next ch-2 sp, ch 1, 3 dc in beg ch-sp, ch 1, dc in 3rd ch of beg ch-4 – four 3-dc groups.

Row 3: Ch 4 (counts as dc, ch 1), turn, 3 dc in first ch-1 sp, ch 1, 3 dc in next ch-1 sp, ch 1, (3 dc, ch 2, 3 dc) in next ch-2 sp, ch 1, 3 dc in next ch-1 sp, ch 1, 3 dc in beg ch-sp, ch 1, dc in 3rd ch of beg ch-4 – six 3-dc groups.

Row 4: Ch 4 (counts as dc, ch 1), turn, 3 dc in first ch-1 sp, (ch 1, 3 dc in next ch-1 sp) 2 times, ch 1, (3 dc, ch 2, 3 dc) in next ch-2 sp, (ch 1, 3 dc in next ch-1 sp) 2 times, ch 1, 3 dc in beg ch-sp, ch 1, dc in 3rd ch of beg ch-4 – eight 3-dc groups.

Rows 5-32: Ch 4 (counts as dc, ch 1), turn, 3 dc in first ch-1 sp, *ch 1, 3 dc in next ch-1 sp; rep from * to center ch-2 sp, ch 1, (3 dc, ch 2, 3 dc) in center ch-2 sp, **ch 1, 3 dc in next ch-1 sp; rep from ** to beg ch-sp, ch 1, 3 dc in beg ch-sp, ch 1, dc in 3rd ch of beg ch-4 – sixty-four 3-dc groups in row 32.

Fasten off.

Join B with a sl st in last st of Row 32.

Rows 33-47: Rep Row 5 – ninety-four 3-dc groups in Row 47.

Fasten off.

FINISHING

Fringe

Cut 2 strands each of A and B about 12" (30.5 cm) long. Hold the 4 strands of yarn together and fold in half. Use crochet hook to draw fold through ch-sp at edge of piece, forming a loop. Pull ends of fringe through this loop, then pull to tighten.

Make a fringe in each ch-sp along lower edge of Shawl. Trim fringe evenly.

Weave in ends.

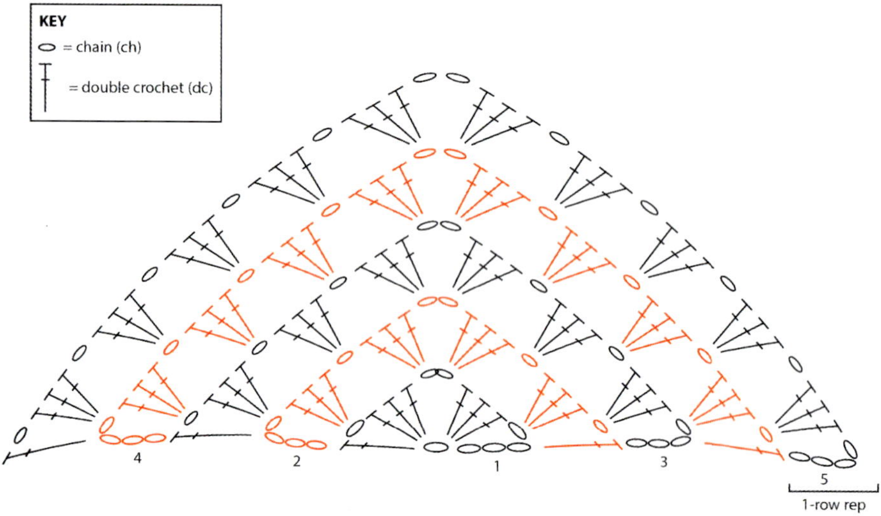

FRODE SHAWL

BASIC

SIZE

About 15" x 69" (38 cm x 175 cm)

GAUGE

8 single crochet = about 4" (10 cm).

BE SURE TO CHECK YOUR GAUGE.

SHOPPING LIST

BULKY 5

Yarn (Bulky Weight)
LION BRAND® HOMESPUN® NEW LOOK (Art. #575)
☐ #621 Mountain View - 3 cakes

Crochet Hook
LION BRAND® crochet hook
☐ Size N (10 mm)

Additional Supply
☐ LION BRAND® large-eyed blunt needle

NOTES

1. Shawl is worked lengthwise in one piece.

SHAWL

Chain 138.

Row 1: Single crochet in 2nd chain from hook and in each chain across – 137 stitches at the end of this row.

Rows 2-4: Chain 1, turn, single crochet in each stitch across.

Row 5: Chain 4 (counts as double crochet and 1 chain-1 space), turn, skip first 2 stitches, double crochet in next stitch, *chain 1, skip next stitch, double crochet in next stitch; repeat from * across – 69 double crochet and 68 chain-1 spaces at the end of this row.

Row 6: Chain 1, turn, single crochet in first double crochet, *single crochet in next chain-1 space, single crochet in next double crochet; repeat from * across to turning chain-space, single crochet in turning chain-space, single crochet in 3rd chain of turning chain – 137 stitches.

Rows 7-13: Chain 1, turn, single crochet in each stitch across.

Rows 14-31: Repeat Rows 5-13 twice more.

Rows 32 and 33: Repeat Rows 5 and 6.

Rows 34-36: Chain 1, turn, single crochet in each stitch across.

Fasten off.

FINISHING

Weave in ends.

ULRICA SHAWL

BASIC

SIZE

About 16" x 72" (40.5 cm x 183 cm)

GAUGE

12 hdc = about 4" (10 cm).

BE SURE TO CHECK YOUR GAUGE.

SHOPPING LIST

Yarn (Medium Weight) MEDIUM 4

LION BRAND® LANDSCAPES® (Art. #545)

☐ #220 Twilight - 6 balls

Crochet Hook

LION BRAND® crochet hook

☐ Size K-10.5 (6.5 mm) **or** size needed for gauge

Additional Supplies

☐ LION BRAND® large-eyed blunt needle

☐ 5" x 5" (12.5 cm x 12.5 cm) piece of cardboard

NOTES

1. Shawl is worked in one piece, back and forth in rows.

2. The tassels are worked first, so that you can use all of the remaining yarn for the Shawl.

TASSELS (MAKE 4)

Wrap yarn around cardboard 40 times. Cut a 15" (38 cm) length of yarn and thread into blunt needle. Draw needle under all strands at upper edge of cardboard. Pull tightly and knot securely near strands. Don't trim the tying strand – you'll need it to tie the tassel to your Shawl. Cut yarn loops at lower edge of cardboard. Cut another length of yarn and wrap tightly around loops 1" (2.5 cm) below top knot.
Knot securely; thread ends into needle and weave into center of tassel.
Trim tassel ends evenly.

SHAWL

Ch 50.

Row 1: Hdc in 3rd ch from hook and in each ch across.

Row 2: Ch 2, turn, hdc in each st across, work last hdc in top of turning ch.

Rep Row 2 until almost all yarn has been used.

Fasten off.

FINISHING

Tie a tassel to each corner of the Shawl.

Weave in yarn ends.

GRETEL MITTS

EASY

SIZES

Finished Circumference:
8" (20.5 cm)

Finished Length:
8" (20.5 cm)

GAUGE

16 hdc and 14 rnds = about 4 in. (10 cm).

BE SURE TO CHECK YOUR GAUGE.

SHOPPING LIST

Yarn (Medium Weight) MEDIUM 4

LION BRAND® FEELS LIKE BUTTA (Art. #215)

- ☐ #108 Dusty Blue - 1 ball (A)
- ☐ #178 Teal - 1 ball (B)

Crochet Hook

LION BRAND® crochet hook

- ☐ Size G-6 (4 mm)
  or size needed for gauge

Additional Supply

- ☐ LION BRAND® large-eyed blunt needle

NOTES

1. Mitts are worked in the round, then back and forth in rows to shape the thumbhole.

2. Mitts are worked with 2 colors of yarn. To change yarn color, work last st of old color to last yarn over. Yarn over with new color and draw through all loops to complete st. Proceed with new color. Fasten off old color.

MITTS (MAKE 2)

With A, ch 32. Join with sl st in first ch to make a ring, being careful not to twist.

Rnd 1: Ch 2 (counts as first hdc in this rnd and all following rnds), hdc in each ch around, join with sl st in top of beg ch-2 – you'll have 32 hdc.

Rnds 2-10: Ch 2, hdc in each st around; join with sl st in top of beg ch-2.

Change to B.

Rnds 11-18: With B, ch 2, hdc in each st around; join with sl st in top of beg ch-2.

THUMBHOLE

Note: The thumbhole is worked back and forth in rows.

Rows 1-6: Ch 2 (counts as hdc), TURN, hdc in each st across. Do NOT join.

Join to continue in the round.

Next Rnd: With B, ch 2, hdc in each st around, join with sl st in top of beg ch-2.

Last 3 Rnds: Ch 2, hdc in each st around; join with sl st in top of beg ch-2.

Fasten off.

FINISHING

Weave in ends.

GENERAL INSTRUCTIONS

ABBREVIATIONS

beg = begin(ning)(s)
ch = chain
ch-sp(s) = chain space(s) previously made
cm = centimeters
dc = double crochet
hdc = half double crochet
mm = millimeters
rem = remain(ing)(s)
rep(s) = repeat(s)
rnd(s) = round(s)
RS = right side
sc = single crochet
sk = skip
sl st = slip stitch
sp(s) = space(s)
st(s) = stitch(es)
tr = treble (triple) crochet
WS = wrong side

CROCHET TERMINOLOGY		
UNITED STATES		INTERNATIONAL
slip stitch (slip st)	=	single crochet (sc)
single crochet (sc)	=	double crochet (dc)
half double crochet (hdc)	=	half treble crochet (htr)
double crochet (dc)	=	treble crochet (tr)
treble crochet (tr)	=	double treble crochet (dtr)
double treble crochet (dtr)	=	triple treble crochet (ttr)
triple treble crochet (tr tr)	=	quadruple treble crochet (qtr)
skip	=	miss

CROCHET HOOKS	
U.S.	Metric mm
B-1	2.25
C-2	2.75
D-3	3.25
E-4	3.5
F-5	3.75
G-6	4
7	4.5
H-8	5
I-9	5.5
J-10	6
K-10½	6.5
L-11	8
M/N-13	9
N/P-15	10
P/Q	15
Q	16
S	19

* or ** — When you see an asterisk used within a pattern row or round, the symbol indicates that later you will be told to repeat a portion of the instruction. Most often the instructions will say, repeat from * or ** so many times.

( ) or [ ] — Sets off a short number of stitches that are repeated or indicates additional information.

- When you see - (dash) followed by a number of stitches, this tells you how many stitches you will have at the end of a row or round.

BASIC	Projects using basic stitches. May include basic increases and decreases.
EASY	Projects may include simple stitch patterns, color work, and/or shaping.
INTERMEDIATE	Projects may include involved stitch patterns, color work, and/or shaping.
COMPLEX	Projects may include complex stitch patterns, color work, and/or shaping using a variety of techniques and stitches simultaneously.

GAUGE

Never underestimate the importance of gauge. Achieving the correct gauge assures that the finished size of your piece matches the finished size given in the pattern.

CHECKING YOUR GAUGE

Work a swatch that is at least 4" (10 cm) square. Use the suggested hook size and the number of stitches given. If your swatch is larger than 4" (10 cm), you need to work it again using a smaller hook; if it is smaller than 4" (10 cm), try it with a larger hook. This might require a swatch or two to get the exact gauge given in the pattern.

METRICS

As a handy reference, keep in mind that 1 ounce = approximately 28 grams and 1" = 2.5 centimeters.

TERMS

Fasten off — To end your piece, you need to simply cut and pull the yarn through the last loop left on the hook. This keeps the last stitch intact and prevents the work from unraveling.

Right side — Refers to the front of the piece.

Yarn Weight Symbol & Names	LACE 0	SUPER FINE 1	FINE 2	LIGHT 3	MEDIUM 4	BULKY 5	SUPER BULKY 6	JUMBO 7
Type of Yarns in Category	Fingering, size 10 crochet thread	Sock, Fingering, Baby	Sport, Baby	DK, Light Worsted	Worsted, Afghan, Aran	Chunky, Craft, Rug	Super Bulky, Roving	Jumbo, Roving
Crochet Gauge* Ranges in Single Crochet to 4" (10 cm)	32-42 sts**	21-32 sts	16-20 sts	12-17 sts	11-14 sts	8-11 sts	6-9 sts	5 sts and fewer
Advised Hook Size Range	Steel*** 6 to 8, Regular hook B-1	B-1 to E-4	E-4 to 7	7 to I-9	I-9 to K-10½	K-10½ to M/N-13	M/N-13 to Q	Q and larger

*GUIDELINES ONLY: The chart above reflects the most commonly used gauges and hook sizes for specific yarn categories.

** Lace weight yarns are usually crocheted with larger hooks to create lacy openwork patterns. Accordingly, a gauge range is difficult to determine. Always follow the gauge stated in your pattern.

*** Steel crochet hooks are sized differently from regular hooks–the higher the number, the smaller the hook, which is the reverse of regular hook sizing.

We have made every effort to ensure that these instructions are accurate and complete. We cannot, however, be responsible for human error, typographical mistakes, or variations in individual work.

Copyright © 2019 by Leisure Arts, Inc., 104 Champs Blvd., STE 100, Maumelle, AR 72113-6738, www.leisurearts.com. All rights reserved. This publication is protected under federal copyright laws. Reproduction or distribution of this publication or any other Leisure Arts publication, including publications which are out of print, is prohibited unless specifically authorized. This includes, but is not limited to, any form of reproduction or distribution on or through the Internet, including posting, scanning, or e-mail transmission.

©2019 Lion Brand Yarn Company, all rights reserved.

Made in U.S.A.